Shelly's
Outdoor
Adventure

by Kentrell Martin

illustrations by Marc Rodriguez

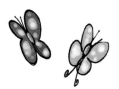

To the Reader

Throughout the book, Shelly's hands demonstrate how each highlighted word is signed. You will find an alphabet chart at the end of the book. A DVD that provides live interpreter guidance is also available from Shelly's Adventures LLC.

Available now:
> *Shelly's Outdoor Adventure*
> *Shelly Goes to the Zoo*

Coming soon:
> *Shelly Visits Washington, D.C.*
> *Shelly Babysits her Baby Brother*
> *Shelly Goes to the Dentist*

Shelly's Outdoor Adventure by Kentrell Martin
Also in the Shelly's Adventures Series: *Shelly Goes to the Zoo*

ISBN: 978-0-9851845-2-0 (hard cover)
ISBN: 978-0-9851845-0-6 (soft cover)
Library of Congress Control Number: 2012902758

First printed in 2013. Reprinted in 2015, 2017, 2018 and 2019.

Published by Shelly's Adventures LLC, PO BOX 2632, Land O Lakes, Fl 34639 USA
Website: www.shellysadventuresllc.com

Printed and bound in the USA

Book design by Jill Ronsley, www.suneditwrite.com

Shelly's Adventures LLC was created to provide children and their parents with reading material that teaches American Sign Language. Shelly's Adventures LLC produces materials that make signing fun for kids, parents and teachers.

Hello. My name is Shelly.
Today my friends and I are planning a walk. Along the way, I'm going to teach them new signs.

"It's a beautiful day," says Shelly.
"It sure is, Shelly!" says Amber.
"There is hardly a cloud in the sky."

Shelly looks up. "Yes! Did you see how bright the sun is?" She turns towards Amber and signs SUN.

Circle a flattened O hand-shape.
Then bring it downward and open your hand.

"You can tell that fall has come
because the leaves are falling off
the trees," says Shelly as she
signs the word TREE.

Hold up a **5** hand.
Twist it twice.

Amber smiles and says, "I love listening
to the sounds of birds chirping."
Maria winks. "It sounds like they are singing,"
she says.

"Those birds are called mocking birds," says Shelly as she shows them the sign for BIRD.

Place your hand at the side of your mouth. Open and close the thumb and index finger twice.

"Look at those butterflies," Shelly says, pointing at the colorful winged creatures. She signs BUTTERFLY.

Show a butterfly and flap your hands twice.

"They are beautiful!" says Amber.

"Maria, did you know that butterflies come from caterpillars?"

Maria replies, "I didn't know that."

Maria notices a flowerbed and says,
"Look! Flowers! I'm going to pick some
to take home to my mother."
"Me, too!" says Amber. She skips to the flowerbed.
"Me three! I love the scent of flowers," says Shelly.

She sniffs the blossoms and shows her friends the sign for FLOWER.

Move the **O**-shaped hand from one side of your cheek to the other.

All of a sudden, a cat darts past the girls. Maria jumps back and says, "Whoa! That cat scared me. It ran by as if it was in a race."

"Yes, that cat looked very scared," says Shelly. "Maybe it was running away from something." She signs CAT.

Place the "open F" handshape near the bottom of your nose and pull it outward like you are pulling a whisker.

Amber jumps up and shouts, "You're right, Shelly! That cat was running away from something." Two large dogs bolt past them.

Shelly says, "Those are very big dogs!
No wonder the cat was running so fast!"
She signs DOG to Maria and Amber.

Slap hand against leg and
then snap your fingers.

The girls continue their walk.
A few yards ahead, Shelly
stops abruptly.
"Hey! Did you feel that?"
she says, holding out her hand
and looking up to the sky.
"Feel what?" says Maria.

A moment later, the rain starts falling. "Here comes the rain!" says Shelly. She shows them the sign RAIN before they run for cover.

Move your hands down as if your hands are the rain.

A few minutes later, the rain stops and the sky is blue again.
Amber points up and says, "Look at that!"
"What is it?" says Maria.

Amber waves her arm in the air and says, "Over there!"
"Wow! That's a rainbow," says Shelly
as she signs RAINBOW.

Sign color and then move your hand with the four shape in a half circle like the shape of a rainbow.

"I think it's time for us to turn back," says Maria.
"I think you're right," says Amber.

Touch your cheek at the
side of your mouth and
then move your hand
toward your ear.

Shelly looks at her friends and says,
"Come on! Let's go HOME!"
She signs home and they all walk happily
back to their houses.

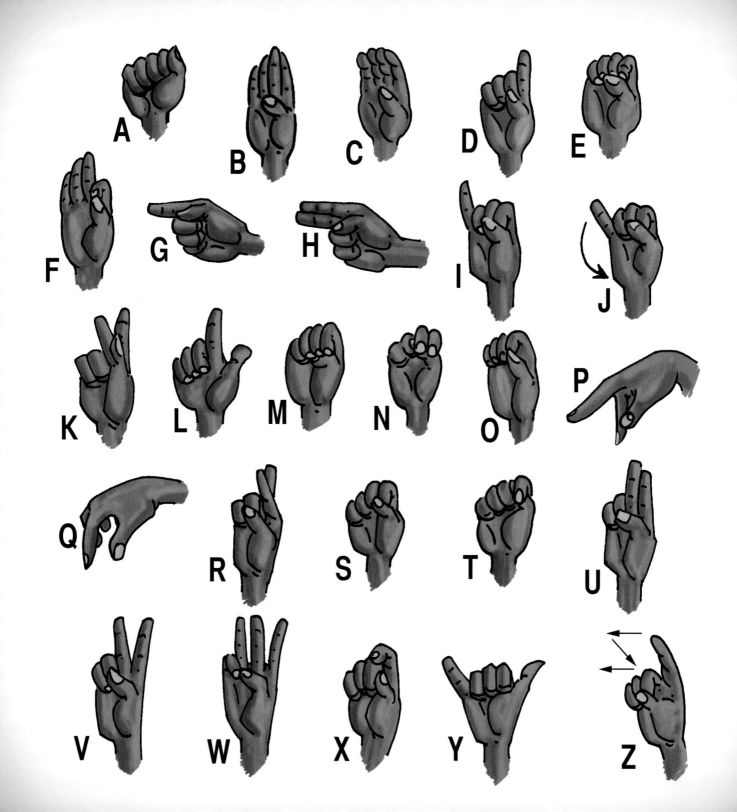